Orpheus in the Undershirt

Kevin Densley

Orpheus in the Undershirt

Acknowledgements

Poems in this book have appeared, sometimes in different form, in the following publications: *Antipodes* (USA), *core*, *FourW*, *Griffith Review*, *The Journal* (UK), *LiNQ*, *Mattoid*, *Monkey Kettle* (UK), *Other Poetry* (UK), *Platform*, *Polestar*, *Quadrant*, *Southerly* and *Tamba*.
Thanks to the editors of these publications.

Also, a big thank-you to Terry Matassoni for the cover art.

Orpheus in the Undershirt
ISBN 978 1 76041 501 3
Copyright © text Kevin Densley 2018
Cover image: detail from *Orpheus in the Undershirt* (2017), by Terry Matassoni, oil on linen, 41 cm by 61 cm

First published 2018 by
GINNINDERRA PRESS
PO Box 3461 Port Adelaide 5015 Australia
www.ginninderrapress.com.au

Contents

Mickey Mouse's Cranial Vault	7
For Shantelle	8
Sequence of Unease	9
Lal Lal, Victoria	10
Virginia Woolf's Manx Cat	11
To Clarissa	12
Iris	13
Martha Graham, 1931	14
Michelangelo Antonioni's *Il Deserto Rosso*	15
Handel's Father was a Barber-surgeon	16
Jack Bradshaw and 'Lovely' Riley	17
A Little Night Music	20
A Poem (Almost) Writes Itself	21
Souvenir Postcard, Photographed by Mr Henry Poil…	22
Late-in-life Photo of Captain Albert Jacka…	23
The Valley of the Shadow of	24
Poses of Languor	26
What Happened at University This Week	27
Lunch with Terrie and Bernadette	28
In Celebration of Great Australian Racehorses	29
Three Photographs from the Early Life of Frances Scott…	34
Shapeshifter	36
Côte d'Azur	37
Not in Praise of Limestone	38
Death of Presley	39
Triptych	40
Beautiful Submerged Things	42
Bushranger Harry Power	43
The Wilful Murder of Constable Samuel Nelson…	45
A Notable Colonial Fistfight…	47

Quietly Neurotic Domestic Interior	54
Journey into the Underworld	55
Striking Out	56
When Johnstone's Circus Came to Town	57
Men of 'Fifty-four	60
Erasmus Fell	61
The Decline of Western Civilisation	62
Death of a Bantam	63

Mickey Mouse's Cranial Vault

Once, I saw in a book
a series of drawings to scale,
showing, decade by decade,
the increasing size
of Mickey Mouse's cranial vault.
Over the years, cartoonists
drew his head bigger
in accordance with the mouse
American people wanted.
First, there was the sassy,
small-headed *Steamboat Willie* mouse
of the late nineteen-twenties,
an era of boundless self-confidence
and insouciant swagger.
But then came Depression,
after that, a world war.
Each time, in response,
Mickey's head grew larger;
the country needed a more cuddly,
big-headed mouse
to clutch to its collective bosom.
So it has gone through the decades…
No surprise that now
the famous rodent's head
is like a giant balloon.

For Shantelle

We stood there,
regarding
skeletal
mist-enshrouded
trees
– what the fuck,
it was all so
poetic,
wasn't it?
You waxed lyrical,
misquoted Yeats.
I corrected
your mistake.
We bought some beers.
Funny,
when we threw
the empty cans
into the canyon,
we never heard them land.

Sequence of Unease

for Richard Cotter

black-and-white images return

man on deserted beach
ashen-grey winter

clump of driftwood,
pointy, twisted,
half-buried in sand

man picks up driftwood
takes it home
puts it on desk in study
vast library surrounds him

now wearing horn-rimmed glasses,
smoky pipe in mouth,
man examines driftwood
from many angles
through enormous magnifying glass

'Early Neolithic,'
he asserts
in this better than average
student film,
made long ago by a male friend,
surprisingly lacking young women's breasts

Lal Lal, Victoria

Smoke from chimneys
of forest houses.
Chilly winter morning
in the township near the waterfall.

A local cat
waits with its mistress
at the V-Line bus stop
as it always does.

Bloke is standing outside the pub
in T-shirt, shorts and boots,
blowing perfect cigarette rings
into the frosty air.

Virginia Woolf's Manx Cat

From my window
I can see her walking
across the quad
at a leisurely pace,
yes there she goes
her head held high,
oblivious
to the dons and beadles who hurry by
to lectures on Browne
and meetings of choral societies.
This Manx cat
is well aware
of the rare feline that she is.
She has no time
for the daily round
going on about her
or for seven-hundred-year-old places
of Western learning.
She's content to pad along,
proud and aloof,
entirely happy
with the pleasure of her own company.

To Clarissa

You didn't know
I saw
the photograph
of you naked,
leaping, arms raised in the air,
into the rock pool on the beach
opposite your house.

Why was this photo
placed on a high ledge
above the basin
in your bathroom?
Anyone small,
or normal height,
wouldn't even see it.
But I'm tall.

Iris

Memories of my grandmother, Dad's mother – connected to shadowy places. Old hotels where we'd counter lunch, ageless crimson carpet on the floor, sunlight filtered through 'Ladies Lounge' stained glass, dust particles in the air, me drinking lemon squashes, or raspberries, eating a plate of fish and chips with a quarter of lemon on the side. Or my family in her backyard late on a summer afternoon beneath a shady pergola covered in gnarled, aged vines. Or I think of the houses where she lived – ancient, dark, high-ceilinged. Enormous padded lounge chairs. In the room with the piano which no one could play, a photo of her de facto, Ken, as a young serviceman heading off to war, bright-eyed and full of hope. He is coughing with emphysema in the next room, the last in a succession of kind-hearted, useless men with whom she shared her life.

Martha Graham, 1931

inspired by a photograph of her taken that year

I can't be bothered
trying to weave
an elaborate metaphor through this poem
to convey the dynamism
of her choreography at the time
and the superlative artistry
with which she moved in space.
I don't have the inclination
to wax lyrical
about her Helen of Troy profile,
long flowing dark hair,
Venus de Miloesque breasts
and powerful, yet lithe, athletic body.
I simply wish to say
in 1931
she had to be
the most desirable woman in the world,
this lady who launched
a thousand dancers and dances.

Michelangelo Antonioni's *Il Deserto Rosso*

the green of the grass is much greener
than it actually would be

the red of her thick winter coat
as she walks across the verdant field
is impossibly red,
contrasting with the blondeness of her hair

she paints her room a different colour
each time she has a change of mood

her upper-middle-class friends
at their weekend bungalow
try aphrodisiacs and talk about sex,
displaying more sophistication
than could be considered credible

as I watch the screen,
I can almost hear the clicking
as the teeth of the sprockets move the film
through the projector

I sense blazing light
passing through celluloid
and wonder why it does not burn,
blacken and curl the print

and Monica Vitti
never looked lovelier

Handel's Father was a Barber-surgeon

Is the guitar obbligato
that old Angus plays
throughout AC-DC's
'Thunderstruck'
essentially Bach's
'Toccata and Fugue'
played backwards?
– Jesus, I hope so.
And is the band's song
'Who Made Who'
the Scottish-Australian lads' contribution
to the Prometheus myth,
à la Shelley's *Frankenstein*?

Jack Bradshaw and 'Lovely' Riley

First, Jack Bradshaw.
Early life:
born Dublin, 1846,
arrived Australia, 1860,
wandered outback New South Wales,
sometime
carnival showman,
farm labourer,
professional foot-runner,
petty thief,
confidence trickster,
complete failure
in early attempts at bank robbery.

'Lovely' Riley:
year of birth: unknown
place of birth: unknown
sometime
professional boxer
other early pursuits: unknown.

Bradshaw teamed with Riley
in the late 1870s
to bungle badly
more robberies.
They were more like a bad vaudeville act
than a duo to be feared.
Example: they captured a bank
in Coolah, New South Wales,
but were driven off empty-handed
by a nurse attending the manager's wife.

Seemingly, their run of outs
ended in May 1880
when they got 2,000 pounds
from the Quirindi bank.
As its manager stabled his horse for the night,
they burst in brandishing pistols
and forced him to open the safe.
But Riley couldn't help bragging
about what the pair had done.
He asked a barber to shave his head
which, he proudly claimed,
would alter his appearance
as he was 'one of the men
who robbed that bank last week'.
When arrested, Bradshaw couldn't conceal
disgust at his muddle-headed mate.
'Riley,' he bemoaned,
'left a trail behind him like a black snake.'
The pair served eight years for their trouble.
The partnership was done.

Jack Bradshaw's later career:
in and out of jail
for various minor crimes
until the new century's early years,
sometime
tent show performer,
'lecturer',
singer and dictator of books,
all based on largely imagined tales
about his bushranging life.

There was hardly a well-known bushranger
he hadn't met, or ridden with,
or didn't know the 'true facts' about.
Towards the end, he believed
his own vivid mythology.
He died in a Sydney nursing home
in the 1930s.

'Lovely' Riley:
later career: unknown
year of death: unknown
place of death: unknown.

A Little Night Music

Prowling cats howl,
restless and distressed.

Gravestones – lunar-lit;
ancestors long-deceased.

Chapel's priestly aura;
novenas, candles, gold.

Limpid light of moon and stars
turning toward love.

A Poem (Almost) Writes Itself

The muse does not descend from high
to whisper felicities
into my ear; instead,
a voice comes from within,
a tranquil, unencumbered place,
compelling me to scrawl.
Later, of course, words may be changed,
lines crossed out, whole stanzas might go:
the process isn't pure.

Now, this morning, gazing
at backyard flowers, sunlit
and hazy hemisphere of sky,
I invoke my inner muse.
Let the channel open.

Souvenir Postcard, Photographed by Mr Henry Poil, Wangaratta, Victoria, 9 April 1865

Mad Dan Morgan – dead –
propped up in a chair,
dirty curly black hair and beard,
eyes opened, Colt revolver
placed in his right hand…

After the posthumous 'sitting',
his beard was flayed from his face,
head shaved then hacked off,
tossed round the room
by exuberant police,
rolled on the floor
like a bowling ball,
then soaked in salt water
and wrapped in hessian.
Unsurprisingly, it arrived
in Professor Halford's hands
at Melbourne University
in too poor condition
for scientific study.

Late-in-life Photo of Captain Albert Jacka (1893–1932) VC, MC and Bar

Monochrome day,
'28 or '9.
What season? Winter?
Hard to say.
Jacka sits on a bench
overlooking blustery grey
St Kilda Beach,
his little daughter beside him.
He has aged beyond his years
– wartime illnesses,
gunshot and shrapnel wounds,
mustard gas…

Offshore, the waves,
bleak and black.

The Valley of the Shadow of

(Racecourse Road, Flemington, Melbourne)

Racecourse Road,
the valley of the shadow of
the high-rise housing commission flats.

Racecourse Road,
where Melbourne's cheapest beer can be bought
in any of three supermarkets

(for stupefaction purposes,
the proletariat in the high-rise
need affordable alcohol).

Racecourse Road,
pawnbrokers delight,
but not one of them would buy

my collection of old watches
when I tried to offload them
once, when short of cash.

Hard luck stories abound
on the weary footpaths
of Racecourse Road

as do Chinese restaurants,
halal butchers,
kebab shops

fish-and-chip-and-burger joints
with handwritten meal deals sticky-taped
in their front widows.

Racecourse Road
where homeless alcoholics
drink in the square

or under shady trees
in the nearby park
when the weather is hot.

Racecourse Road,
the valley of the shadow of
the high-rise housing commission flats.

Poses of Languor

Show me women
in poses of languor,
seated on divans with heads tossed back
and backs of pale hands on wearied brows.
Allow them to be full-breasted women
with smooth décolletages.
Clothe them in sumptuous dresses
from Watteau paintings
and bathe them in pools of mellow sunlight
cast through wide bay windows
late in afternoons.
Let turbaned Albanian noblemen
in crimson, gold-embossed uniforms
enter from stage right
and sing them dark-eyed arias
of passionate, undying love.
Let me, for a moment,
lose myself in these scenes.
Let me caress them with my eyes,
for I'm terrified that if I blink
they'll disappear forever.

What Happened at University This Week

Temelza, a fellow tutor,
lost the key to the Red Room
(the place, a couple of days ago,
we had our half-year meeting
and bantered about assessment).
Linda had given the key to Jane
who handed it to Temelza,
who promptly, characteristically,
misplaced the aforesaid thing.
Blithe-spirited Temelza
(who I secretly call Rapunzel
because of her long fair hair
and penchant for fairy tales)
probably doesn't realise now,
more than three days later,
the emails that have passed
about the precious article.
It currently sits in the pocket
of the dress she flung on a rocking chair
as soon as she got home
to put on a favourite jumper and jeans.
It's a serious matter, this missing key:
people want to have meetings,
sit their thoughtful asses
upon the velvet crimson
in this allusive room.

Lunch with Terrie and Bernadette

Carlton
– edgy, alternative theatre,
arty-farty Carlton –
ended in 1983,
around the time I lunched
with the actor and the dancer
in their rented house in Lygon Street.
At a table of Moroccan dips
and chicken wrapped in filo,
we talked in earnest about my play
and their recent show at La Mama,
unaware that the heart
of the world of the nearby streets
– for years, such an edgy,
alternative theatre,
arty-farty zone –
was arteriosclerotic,
or had thudded to a halt.

In Celebration of Great Australian Racehorses

In early colonial racing days,
Australian turf's first champion,
Jorrocks, 'The Iron Horse'
– a winner up to age eighteen –
discovered pulling a dray
on a farm in central New South Wales.

Then *The Barb*,
'The Black Demon',
so-called
for wildness and temper,
winner of the '66 Cup,
a wonder at weight-for-age.

Grand Flaneur, never beaten.
His jockey, Tom Hales,
our greatest nineteenth-century hoop,
described the horse
as a 'smasher'.
Easy winner of the '80 Cup, Victoria and AJC Derbies.

Carbine, son of *Musket*,
'Old Jack',
a bay,
16.1 hands,
a white patch on his left hind leg,
perhaps the greatest of all,

winner of the 1890 Cup
lumping a record weight (10 stone 5)
in a record time (3.28.3)
in a record field
of starters (39).
A character,

the crowd's darling
and when, at the Duke of Portland's stud
in England,
would wander round the property
wearing a hat.
He didn't like his head getting wet.

Next in this Hall of Renown, *Newhaven*.
Won the '96 Cup by six lengths,
trained by Carbine's man, Hickinbotham,
who refused to say which was the better horse.
'I didn't know how good Newhaven was,' he said,
'because I never saw him extended.'

Manfred,
possibly the most
naturally talented
of the lot
but wayward and temperamental.
Missed the start of the AJC Derby

by 100 yards
but got up to win by a neck.
Jockey Lewis once said
that when the horse was in the mood
'you could ride him
with a piece of cotton'.

Then *Phar Lap*,
'The Red Terror',
the icon,
17.1 hands,
a heart
twice the normal size;

like Bradman, an idol of the Depression,
victorious in Mexico's
Agua Caliente Handicap,
then the world's richest race,
winning it in a canter.
He tragically died weeks later.

Tulloch,
as a three-year-old
doubtless the finest thoroughbred
on the planet,
struck down with illness at his peak,
spent eighteen months

lying against the wall of his barn.
Tommy Smith, his trainer, said,
'I thought that he would die for sure.'
But Tulloch returned
to the track again,
retiring a champion.

Kingston Town,
'The Black Horse',
won his third Cox Plate
from a hopeless place in the field.
He lurched around Melbourne's
left-handed tracks

'like a good-natured drunk',
according to caller Bill Collins,
yet was still,
in spite of the way of going,
many times
victorious there.

Might and Power,
for a glorious year,
the finest stayer in the world.
At his peak would have won
the Prix de l'Arc de Triomphe
by three lengths pulling up.

Of the 1997 Caulfield Cup,
my racehorse-owning barber said,
concerning this horse's stunning
seven length win:
'He could easily
have gone round again.'

In more recent times, *Sunline, Northerly,
Makybe Diva, Black Caviar…*

A joyful salute
to these equine immortals!

Three Photographs from the Early Life of Frances Scott Fitzgerald Lanahan Smith (1921–1986)

There you are,
coyly smiling,
only two years old,
hand in hand
with your father and mother,
high kicking in front of a Christmas tree,
typical expatriate
Americans in Paris
– hardly –
Scott writing *Gatsby*,
battling with his drinking,
Zelda madly practising,
far too late,
to be a ballerina.

In another photo
taken when you're seven,
the three of you are in the shallows
at a beach on the Côte d'Azur:
Zelda in a stylish one-piece,
Scottie in the middle, paddling,
Scott lounging on the other side,
protectively near his daughter.
Possibly Gerald and Sara Murphy,
that highly glamorous pair,
sat watching from the sand,
the couple who invented sunbathing,

at least in the form
in which it has come down to us
in the Western world.

Fast forward to your Vassar
graduation portrait:
a pretty blonde twenty-one-year-old
with the fine features of her father,
two years dead,
and the darker mystery of her mother,
now locked behind an asylum's walls.
One could be forgiven
for wondering about the baggage
resulting from such parents
– Scott and Zelda, patron saints
of the decadent Jazz Age –
but instead their daughter wrote
of her childhood as idyllic,
to use her own word, *golden*.

Shapeshifter

Now square-shouldered,
wearing suit coat

Now as fluid,
in outline, as ghost

Now circular,
like lower-case 'o'

Now pretzel-thin
– swizzle stick mode

Côte d'Azur

Young woman
in a summer dress
and broad sun hat – both white –

stands
upon a bleached stone
balcony –

facing
azure sky,
sweep of sea –

white haze –

Not in Praise of Limestone

Gneiss is much gneisser.

Death of Presley

The King died on the dunny,
his silk pyjamas ankle-low.
Just underlines the old saying, I guess
– when you've got to go, you've got to go.

Triptych

after Ingrès, *La Grande Odalisque*

In the first panel, we can see
the odalisque naked upon the divan.
She's a strapping woman,
like Ingrès' *La Grande*,
and, similarly, our view of her
is from behind.
Notice the long and sensual curve
of her back,
the alabaster lustre of her skin,
the ripe firmness of the visible breast
and, just within reach of her hand,
on the parquet,
a biodegradable brown-paper bag
upon which is a symbol known
throughout the world.
The bag contains a cheeseburger
with sugary sauce
and a thin slice of pickle.

In the second panel, you will observe
that the odalisque has raised the treat
to her lips,
and is just about to part them and bite
into it.
Look at her long, fleshy arm.
Observe her large fingers and hand.
See the tiny drop of red (it's sauce)
on the green velvet she lounges upon.

Notice that the slice of cheese
in the bun she is holding
has curled its corners up,
as if it is rejecting
the burger underneath it.

Now we've come to the final panel
– a stark, horrible sight.
See the head tossed back,
the mouth agape,
the open, vacant, gelatinous eyes.
Note the burger on the polished floor
with a single bite taken out of it.
Observe that now the odalisque
is flat on her back;
both arms hang limply,
her heavy breasts have begun to sag
and her fingertips
touch lightly upon the parquetry.

Beautiful Submerged Things

Shakespeare's Ophelia
drowned.
Painted by Millais
– floating hair, wildflowers.

Virginia Woolf
drowned.
Put stones in her pockets,
breasted the stream.

Sylvia Plath,
in 'Lorelei',
yearned to be ferried
down there.

Full fathom five
thy father lies…

Bushranger Harry Power

(Henry Johnson 1819–1891)

Harry Power was a blusterer
who robbed with threats
he'd never have carried out.
He would turn from intended victims
and pray out loud, theatrically,
'Please Lord,
let this fellow give me his goods,
for I do not wish to shoot him.'
Though Harry, it must be said,
was always polite to women,
showering them with elaborate,
old-fashioned compliments.
He would play upon his age.
'I hope you'll excuse me madam,' he'd say,
while pocketing their jewellery.
'I'm just an old man
trying to make a living.'
He was also a great bushman, horseman,
in spite of painful bunions
and irritable bowels,
and claimed credit for teaching
a young Ned Kelly
the art of bushranging life,
reportedly saying at one hold-up,
nodding towards the nervous boy,
'Excuse the lad,
he's only learning the game.'

But later, Old Harry never lost a chance
to criticise his apprentice,
many said because the latter
became much better known.

Though comical in many ways,
Harry Power was a survivor:
youthful convict in Van Diemen's Land,
Victorian goldfields raconteur,
hard time in the hulks and Pentridge,
then bushranging in the High Country,
followed by yet another stretch
attending the Bluestone College.
Finally, Harry got an honest job
telling lies as 'the oldest living bushranger'
aboard the prison hulk *Success*
which had become a museum.
Tourists flocked to see him,
and he loved being centre-stage.
But, on holidays, near Swan Hill,
he fell into the Murray and drowned,
hardly a fitting conclusion
for a colourful show-off like Harry,
'the man who taught Ned Kelly'.

The Wilful Murder of Constable Samuel Nelson by Johnny Dunn of Ben Hall's Gang, Main Street, Collector, New South Wales, 26 January 1865

In the gloaming,
suddenly gunfire.
A hold-up at Kimberley's Inn.
'Hall's Gang,' Nelson declared.
He leapt up from the table.
'I was told they'd pay a visit.'
Mrs Nelson begged, implored her husband,
'No! Don't go!'
She tugged at the constable's sleeve
as he buttoned up his tunic.
'I must, and will, do my duty.'
He disappeared out the door,
her arms flailing in his wake.
Gamely, he hurried up Main Street,
fixed a bayonet to his carbine.
Johnny Dunn, on the hotel veranda,
look-out for Gilbert and Hall,
saw Nelson approach
and stage-whispered, 'Police!'
Inside, Hall,
'You can handle it, Jack!'
Unseen by the constable,
Dunn disappeared
behind the pub's side fence.

'Stand!' he yelled, jumping up
as Nelson
drew within ten yards,
at the same time firing his revolver.
The policeman fell
– a gaping wound
to the side of the head.
Blood mingled with the dust.
Dunn ran into the open,
pumped another bullet
into the dying man.
Gilbert and Hall, hearing the shots,
ran outside to see.
A whispered conversation
between the three gang members.
Gilbert removed the policeman's belt.
'I need one of these,' he smirked.
The bushrangers galloped away,
soon pursued by a party
of troopers scouting nearby.
Shots were exchanged.
But the Hall Gang's horses were faster
and the night was very dark.
The policemen returned to Collector,
their quarry as elusive
and wild as the wind.

A Notable Colonial Fistfight: Edward 'Ned' Kelly vs Isaiah 'Wild' Wright, Beechworth, Victoria, 8 August 1874

Saturday afternoon
in the Imperial Hotel.
Regulars. Laughter.
A squeeze box. An old man
dances a stiff-jointed jig.
Alone by the window, Kelly
sips on an ale,
gazing at High Street's passing parade.
A stocky, bull-necked man walks by,
jolting him out of his reverie.
'Bloody Wright!'
Wild enters the bar.
Kelly turns, glares.
Words fly.
About a stolen horse
– Isaiah Wright: sentence eighteen months,
for illegally using, not stealing;
Edward Kelly: sentence three years,
for receiving the same beast,
though he didn't know it was stolen.
Wild hadn't bothered to tell him that.
Ned also hadn't forgotten
the arrest by Senior Constable Hall
– helped by others, the bloated Scot
had tried to kill him.
(His mother was certainly right
when she told him as a boy,
'The police have it in for our lot, son.')

This is the first occasion
Ned and Wild have seen each other
since doing time.
Kelly rises from his stool, fists clenched.
Wright, a notorious fighter,
calmly stands his ground.
'All right, Ned. If that's what you want…'
The sporty publican, Rogers,
a well-known organiser
of wrestling bouts, fist fights, cricket and skittles,
nimbly steps in.
'Gentleman, gentlemen!
No fighting in here.
If you really want to settle this…'
He outfits the combatants
in boxing attire
– white singlets, silk shorts, lightweight shoes –
then calls to his offsider,
'Take over. I may be some time.'
Rogers, the two men and half the pub
proceed to the sporting ground
on the banks of Spring Creek,
below the fruit and hop garden.
Others join them along the way.
Rogers takes centre stage.

He extends his arms,
establishing distance between the two men,
both physically impressive,
particularly for the time:
Kelly, age nineteen, six feet tall, twelve stone;
Wright, twenty-five, five-eleven, a stone and a half heavier.
The spectators, wide-eyed, expectant,
form an enthusiastic circle.
Among them, many faces familiar
to Kelly and Wright: Brickey Williamson,
Joe Byrne, Aaron Sherritt, Tom Lloyd…
Rogers holds forth.
'The Old London Rules, gentlemen.
No Marquis of Queensberry here!'
The crowd cheer loudly.
Eyes locked, the two men nod.
Rogers flourishes a stick
then draws a line in the dirt.
'Mr Kelly and Mr Wright
– to the mark!'

Wild charges forward, swinging.
His first punch,
a roundhouse right,
would have knocked a man's head off
if it had connected.

Kelly, watchful, sees it coming and ducks.
Wright swishes the air.
Ned's first blow,
a short right to the solar plexus,
is thrown from the heels.
Wild doubles over, lets out a groan,
for his trouble gets two jabs to the head.
He stumbles back, hands up, blinking,
trying to clear his vision.
He smiles.
Fighters always smile
when they know they're in trouble.
Momentarily, he sees two Neds.
One will be plenty.
For much of the round, they stalk each other,
feinting and throwing inquiring jabs.
Wild tries another haymaker
but it misses by two feet.
A straight left from Ned to the nose draws blood.
End of Round One.
The next few rounds.
Ned, more scientific, picks off the shorter, stockier Wild
with stinging jabs.
Then Wild, veteran of many battles,
starts to fight more cleverly,
no longer recklessly swinging
and leaving himself an easy target.
He looks for openings,
once lands a good left hook
but Ned doesn't even flinch.

It is like hitting a block of granite.
'I'll be in for a long afternoon,' thinks Wild.
The middle rounds see Wild
increasingly desperate.
He tries to put Ned off,
uses everything
in his pugilist's bag of tricks.
He points to his chin,
drops his hands,
sways his head in and out of range,
yells distracting comments to the crowd:
'I've got him now!'
'He's starting to look worried.' (He isn't.)
Nothing works.
Ned pursues him relentlessly,
not allowing his concentration
to be broken for a second.
The later rounds.
Thwack thwack thwack!
The jabs keep coming.
To Ned, it is like chopping down a tree.
The time in Gippsland, swinging an axe,
breaking bluestone in Williamstown
stand him in good stead.
All the right muscles are finely tuned,
his instincts sharply honed.
Wild still connects occasionally,
to little effect.

He tries to rally
but the stable doors have closed
and the horse has long since bolted.
In the last rounds, Wild
clinches and wrestles,
the only way he can survive.
'Come on boys! Is this a fight
or the Pride of Erin?'
yells Aaron Sherritt,
who can't resist getting off a good line,
whatever the circumstances.
Ned catches his eye.
Sherritt shuts up immediately.
The final round.
Ned is raining blows
on a stumbling, defeated Wild.
In the crowd, Wild's deaf-mute brother,
locally nicknamed 'Dummy'
(when Wild isn't around),
moans in great agitation
at seeing his brother's punishment.
It takes three men to prevent him
from leaping into the fray.
Ned throws a wicked right to the chin.
Wild sags to his knees, swaying.
Rogers the publican jumps in,
raises the victor's hand.
'Kelly, the winner in twenty!'
The crowd claps and whistles.
Hats are thrown in the air.

The district has a new champion.
Wild grabs a towel from his 'picker up',
wipes the blood from his face
then pushes through the throng around Ned.
He holds out his hand,
'The better man won.'
Ned shakes it, but doesn't say a word.
Walking back through the fruit trees,
in fading late afternoon light,
Joe Byrne says to Sherritt,
'You fancy yourself, Aaron.
How about next time, you challenge Ned?'
Sherritt laughs.
'I'm not that stupid, Joe.
He'd bloody kill me.'

*

Years later, Wild is fighting
for a travelling boxing troupe.
Charlie the spruiker asks him,
'I hear you fought Ned Kelly.
Behind the big talk and the guns,
could he fight?
I mean, really fight?'
'Could he fight?' replies Wild, half-smiling,
recalling that day long ago.
'He gave me the hiding of my life.'

Quietly Neurotic Domestic Interior

'In the last decades interest in hunger artists has declined considerably.' – Kafka

I won't be having lunch today.
My girlfriend has left me
vegetable soup.
It's in the fridge
but I will not eat it.
I'd need to employ
a bowl, a spoon, a saucepan
and it's too much trouble.
Better to let the kitchen sink
remain in its present state
– pristine, gleaming and empty.

Journey into the Underworld

for Rusty

The Stygian gloom
of your toilet bowl
makes me ask the question:
do I really need
to cross that river?

Striking Out

I strike a match.
She dances naked
within the flame.

In a lather of sweat, to the tom-tom beat,
she makes me hot – then vanishes.

Same old voodoo.

When Johnstone's Circus Came to Town

At an unfashionable seaside resort,
no more than a country town
that happened to be near salt water,
Johnstone's Circus arrived
for its annual summer season,
though most of its well-known family
of spangled, toothy artistes
had long ago died,
replaced by a motley ensemble.
'The Big Top' wasn't big;
more like 'The Medium Top'.
Small tears and gaps in the canvas walls
meant kids and shameless adults
who hadn't bought a ticket
peeped in at the show
or crawled between flaps
to squeeze into the audience.
The tent poles leant on an angle.

*

The ticket box opened. Holidaymakers
and locals piled in.
I wondered – would the banked wooden seating
hold under their weight?
Speakers crackled a fanfare
from the age of Edison
and the Grand Entry Parade began.

An old tiger I had seen,
sullen in a trailer-cage,
came in first,
led by the toupeed ringmaster
in a red lamé suit.
With a long wooden pole,
he tapped the tiger on the rump
to keep it from the crowd
– as if it could be bothered.
Then followed a skinny teenage boy,
pimply, leotarded,
falling off his unicycle
to the tufts of the football ground.
A bent, arthritic clown
(the only original Johnstone),
who should have been in an easy chair
on a veranda somewhere
entered next.
He fumbled fake flowers from his sleeve,
presented a puzzled child
with balloons shaped into a sausage dog
and gibbered jokes at the rest of us.
I couldn't understand a word.
A middle-aged lady and man
in skintight lurex pranced into view
– the tightrope act.
But no danger of them being hurt;
the rope was thick wound steel,
four feet from the ground.

Other performers, animals paraded
– a pair of Shetland ponies,
a man wielding enormous knives,
a camel, a boy
riding a baby elephant.
The show began…
and ended.
The main thing I remember
was a bloke with a stock whip
who selected a 'volunteer',
a sassy blonde teenage girl,
and cracked a cigarette from her mouth.
And the man with the knives wasn't bad,
though he threw his shiny missiles
with flagrant, focused violence
– his shapely blonde assistant
looked pale and terrified.

*

We filed from the tent,
chattering, underwhelmed.
Even as a twelve-year-old boy,
I thought Johnstone's Circus crappy.
But now, three decades later,
its strong whiff of manure
smells richly aromatic.

Men of 'Fifty-four

'But how was it they talked low, and their eyes brightened up, and they didn't look at each other, but away over sunset, and had to get up and walk about, and take a stroll in the cool of the evening when they talked about Eureka?' – Henry Lawson, 'An Old Mate of Your Father's'

I've become an old fart,
haven't I? Lawson's
'An Old Mate of Your Father's'
resonates in my guts,
shivers up my backbone.
It's part of my cultural DNA.
The lingering loss…the loneliness…
I feel like crying
into my bitter beer.

Erasmus Fell

Erasmus fell
off the wall,
near the bed,
almost hitting me on the head.
He looked serene and reflective
while writing a note
in a pad
on a desk
but for some unknown reason
decided to choose
that instant to move.
I could have been injured severely
when he selected his moment,
for the frame around him was heavy
and the glass over him was thick,
but lucky for me he'd resolved to drop
not on my head
but upon Percy Shelley,
who was lying on the carpeted floor
beneath the covers
of one slim volume.

The Decline of Western Civilisation

Helpers in kindergartens are now
'early learning facilitators'.

Greyhounds have become
'elite canine athletes'.

Literature academics
specialise in 'twitter poetry'.

Death of a Bantam

Unexpectedly, she survived the winter,
was wizened, old,
the weight of a crumpled sheet of paper,
all feathers, beak and claws.

Had seen off two generations
of bigger, stronger hens;
shuffled around their legs
at the communal food tray,
pecking at what they'd leave behind.

I'm glad she died
inside the chookhouse,
among the warm chooky smells
of straw and shit,
not out in the muddy yard
on that sodden spring afternoon.

www.ingramcontent.com/pod-product-compliance
Lightning Source LLC
Chambersburg PA
CBHW062201100526
44589CB00014B/1899